Rhododendrons

A Wisley Handbook

Rhododendrons

PETER A. COX

Cassell

The Royal Horticultural Society

THE ROYAL HORTICULTURAL SOCIETY

Cassell Educational Limited
Villiers House, 41/47 Strand
London WC2N 5JE
for the Royal Horticultural Society

First published 1971
Second edition 1985
Third edition, fully revised and reset 1989
Fourth edition 1992

British Library Cataloguing in Publication Data
Cox, Peter A.
   Rhododendrons. – New ed.
   1. Rhododendron
   I. Title
   635.9′3362   SB413.R47
   ISBN 0-304-32018-8

Line drawings by Peter Mennim
Photographs by Peter Cox and Michael Warren

Typeset by Chapterhouse, Formby
Printed in Hong Kong by Wing King Tong Co. Ltd

Cover: a mass of rhododendron hybrids gives a dazzling
display at Glendoick Gardens in Scotland.
p.1: 'Lem's Monarch' is an excellent tall large-flowered
rhododendron.
Back cover: 'Curlew' is perhaps the finest of the Glendoick
yellow dwarf hybrids.
   Photographs by Peter A. Cox
p.2: 'Coccinea Speciosa', a Ghent azalea, dates from the
early nineteenth century.
   Photograph by Michael Warren

Contents

Introduction

There are scarcely any gardens in Britain where at least a few rhododendrons cannot be grown successfully. Provided that some simple cultural practices are carried out, there can be hardly any shrub that gives greater reward for less attention. In favourable localities and in a year of little frost many gardens can have rhododendrons in flower for every month of the year.

To most people the word rhododendron is associated with a medium-sized bush with dark green, shiny evergreen leaves and mauve, pink or red flowers. Only two names are well known, the common R. ponticum, which has naturalised itself over large areas of Britain, and the hybrid 'Pink Pearl', which still remains about the most popular variety. Few realise that the genus Rhododendron includes nearly 1000 species (as found in the wild) and many thousands of hybrids (crosses between either two species or subsequent crossings). These range from dwarf creeping alpines only an inch or two high, to trees up to 80 feet (24 m), often with single trunks. The leaves may vary from $\frac{1}{4}$ inch (0.6 cm) to about 2 feet (60 cm) long, and the flower colours range from near blue to violet, crimson, red, orange, yellow, and white, with many combinations and intermediates of these colours.

Azealeas are included in this great genus. They are divided into several groups and the recent revisions in classification have made some changes. The evergreen or semi-evergreen, so called Japanese azaleas include the familiar indoor pot plants. The second main group contains deciduous species: included here are the well known Mollis and Exbury hybrids.

The main parts of the rest of the genus are split into two, the non-scaly or elepidote species and the scaly or lepidote species. Scales are small disc-like dots found on the leaves and other parts of these plants.

A feature common in several species is the presence of a soft felt-like covering, generally on the undersides of the leaves, which is known as indumentum.

Species vary in the wild. If an extreme variation remains constant, it may be given a subspecific or varietal name, for instance R. rupicola var. chryseum.

Opposite: one of the hybrids of Rhododendron yakushimanum (p.54) which have proved such worthy additions to the garden

Rhododendron campanulatum (p.48), showing the indumentum on the undersurface of the leaves

A seedling of a species which has been raised in cultivation may prove to be of special merit and be given what is known as a cultivar or clonal name. An example is R. *calostrotum* 'Gigha'. A clone can only be propagated vegetatively (that is from cuttings, layers or grafts). Seedlings do not have exactly the same characters as the parents.

Rhododendrons in the wild

WHERE THEY GROW NATURALLY

The huge genus *Rhododendron*, one of the largest in the plant kingdom, grows naturally over large areas of rain-soaked mountains, almost entirely in the northern hemisphere.

Although a few species are sub-tropical and come from damp jungles, the vast majority grow high up in the mountains in the temperate zone, sometimes not far below the snow line.

The species can be divided roughly into two groups, those that come from the sub-tropics or further north (there are no known species in the equivalent areas south of the equator), where distinct summer and winter seasons occur, and those from near the equator, where there is no proper winter resting period. This difference is very important from a garden point of view. The first group comes from a climate fairly similar to our own in Britain, and it is these species and their hybrids which we can grow successfully out-of-doors. The second group cannot endure our cold winters and therefore have to be grown in cool greenhouses. The latter species come mainly from the islands of New Guinea, Borneo, Sumatra and Java and are known as the Vireya (Malesian) rhododendrons.

Unfortunately, not all those species from the temperate regions are hardy throughout Britain. Generally speaking, the higher up the mountains they are found, the hardier they are. The great majority of these temperate species come from the eastern Himalaya, north-east Burma and north-west China, with outliers in Japan, north-east Asia, Turkey and the Causasus, Europe and north America.

WHY ARE THEY FOUND THERE?

Generally speaking, all rhododendrons like similar conditions of soil and of climate. In the temperate regions where they are found wild, there is nearly always an abundance of summer rains or a mist, relatively cool summers and a soil rich in organic matter. This organic matter had built up in conditions where the breakdown of fallen leaves and the rotting of branches as well as herbaceous plant materials is slow. Rhododendrons and their relations, the heathers, vacciniums and others, are highly successful colonisers of this type of habitat. All produce great

Above: the exquisite *Rhododendron souliei* (p.48), a particularly hardy species
Below: despite its very early flowering, *Rhododendron dauricum* (p.49) withstands some frost

Above: *Rhododendron occidentale* (p.60), a North American azalea which flowers in summer
Below: a dense low-growing hardy azalea, *Rhododendron kiusianum* (p.61) bears abundant small flowers in May

Rhododendron christi (p.55), a tender Vireya species from New Guinea for the greenhouse

quantities of seed which generally germinate rapidly in warm, moist situations. The ideal natural seedbed for rhododendrons is moss and it so happens that mosses like a similar habitat.

Rhododendrons in the wild are found growing happily in a great many different situations – the top of trees, cliff ledges, on and amongst boulders, by waterfalls, on rocks in a river, on moorlands and pasture, amongst bamboo, in bogs and in many types of forest. This shows that, given the right climate, rhododendrons are very versatile indeed.

Unfortunately, in Britain we cannot be sure of a snow covering and frequently our worst frosts and cold winds occur when the ground is bare, causing damage to the unprotected plants. In the wild at high altitudes, every advantage is taken of any shelter available from rocks and boulders and hollows. The same applies to shade, especially in the heavy monsoon areas, where mist and the rain prevail throughout the growing season. Here we may have several weeks of hot sunny weather. It might be said that prolonged spells of sunshine are rare, but when they do come they can take their toll, especially of anything newly planted. Those species which grow naturally in full exposure in the drier parts of north-west China can take and enjoy nearly full sun in any part of Britain, but most others appreciate a little shade at least during the hottest part of the day.

Preparing for planting

FINDING A SITE

In these days of small suburban houses, few people have much choice of site for their gardening, although many have a plot both in front of and behind the house, giving at least a different exposure to the elements. Those with an acre or two of garden will probably have a few established trees, and in time it might be possible to create both a woodland garden and a rock or peat garden. The combination of these two types of garden enables one to grow successfully a very large range of rhododendrons.

Before planting rhododendrons, there are a few basic factors which must be considered. Firstly, the existing soil and its drainage. Rhododendrons are notorious for their dislike of soils rich in lime. If it is a heavy clay, or at all alkaline, it is no use expecting to grow rhododendrons planted directly into these soils. Beware of beds near walls which may contain lime. With the use of carefully constructed raised beds (see pp.17–18), a collection of small varieties may be grown successfully. With adequate preparation, lighter soils of an acid nature should grow rhododendrons well, provided a little shelter and shade is given.

The tall *Rhododendron oreodoxa* (p.47) is fairly tolerant of lime

In a larger garden, where there is a choice of site, avoid hollows where frost might collect. Frost tends to flow like water and gathers at the lowest points. Try to avoid positions where early flowering varieties will catch the early morning sun. It is astonishing how even a few yards can make all the difference between complete destruction of the flowers by frost and no damage at all.

In seaside districts, protection may have to be given against salt spray, which, if severe, can defoliate certain varieties.

Those who garden in heavy rainfall areas, usually near the milder west coast, could try planting the tender species (which grow naturally on trees or rocks) on mossy tree stumps and trunks or on mossy rocks. Perched up above ground level, they make fascinating focal points of interest. Tender varieties can often be grown successfully against a shady wall, especially in the corner of two walls facing north, north-east, or south-west.

IMPROVING THE ENVIRONMENT

Shade

As a general rule, the larger the leaf, the more shade is required, although, of course, there are exceptions. Plants in the sunnier drier parts of the country require the most shade.

For giving shade, oak and Scots pine are amongst the best trees. The oak is especially good as the root system does not rob rhododendrons of much moisture. Beech, together with oak, produces excellent leaf-mould for mulching and feeding, but the beeches cast too deep a shade to plant underneath. Other trees to avoid, where possible, are ash, elm and birch, which have shallow, greedy root systems. Sycamore casts a heavy shade, drops honey-dew from the aphids feeding on the leaves, which then go black with sooty mould, and the seedlings come up by the thousand everywhere. The majority of small-leaved maples, cherries and species of Sorbus, Styrax, Halesia, Cornus and others, make excellent smaller shade trees.

Shelter

In small gardens, shelter is often already provided by walls,

Opposite above: 'Vanessa Pastel' (p.57), a very good hybrid rhododendron for woodland
Below: 'Orange Beauty' (p.64), an evergreen hybrid azalea, growing in light woodland

buildings and hedges, although of course a new building site may be exposed. It is much better, in most circumstances, to try to reduce the velocity of the wind by a permeable barrier, such as a wattle fence, a beech hedge or a narrow belt of trees. Solid walls and shelter belts of close growing conifers tend only to alter the direction of the wind, which often comes around corners or hits the ground again, some yards further on, just as hard as when it hit the barrier. The taller the hedge or shelter belt, the longer the distance behind it which it will shelter. One of the finest tall hedging plants now available is × *Cupressocyparis leylandii,* which does not become too wide and grows very fast. Beech is excellent but slow. *Chamaecyparis lawsoniana* is good, but rather solid.

For coastal areas, sycamore and Sitka spruce stand up well to the blast, as do *Pinus contorta* and *Pinus radiata* and Corsican and Austrian pines. For warmer coastal districts, excellent secondary breaks can be provided by *Griselinia littoralis, Elaeagnus* varieties, *Olearia albida, O. macrodonta, O. traversii* and *Escallonia macrantha* and the larger hybrids.

Plants to associate with rhododendrons

In nature, nearly all rhododendrons are social plants and grow in large colonies, either all one species, or up to several mixed together, sometimes to the exclusion of other genera; in other cases, they may grow in clumps between trees, in a pasture and among other shrubs, or, more rarely, associated with herbaceous plants.

The chief feeding area of rhododendrons is just below the surface of the soil and therefore any other plants growing over the roots compete with them for food and water. Many people advocate planting herbaceous plants along with rhododendrons, but for the reason given above, they are wrong. Well grown rhododendrons should have branches right down to the ground wherever possible. Not only are the roots then shaded by the plant's own foliage, which is beneficial, but the lower branches trap falling leaves which help to mulch and feed naturally. By all means, plant groups of woodland-loving plants in clumps between the rhododendrons, but never *over* their root systems. Plants which associate well in these conditions are related ericaceous shrubs, such as *Vaccinium, Gaultheria, Phyllodoce, Cassiope* species and the larger growing *Pieris* and *Enkianthus.* Then in suitable situations groups of primulas, meconopsis and gentians, lilies, trilliums and erythroniums can be planted.

Dwarf rhododendrons, especially, should be grown socially.

'Dora Amateis' (p.57), a lovely dwarf hybrid rhododendron

Careful grouping of the different leaf colours will maintain an interest even when the plants are not in flower, and it is important to grade the heights, the taller varieties to the back of a border with the lower growing dwarfs planted to give an undulating effect towards the front.

PREPARATION OF THE SOIL

The longer one grows rhododendrons the more one realises that it always pays to prepare the ground adequately beforehand. 'Adequately' means providing conditions in which the roots of rhododendrons can grow happily.

There are two methods of preparation: either dig individual holes, or make a bed to take several plants. If the ground is not naturally full of organic matter and is already loose and friable, as large an area as possible should be prepared for each plant. In other words, prepare enough ground to allow for many years' expansion of the root system. A whole bed is, of course, the best, but there is not always enough room for this.

All rhododendrons require perfect drainage. Under all soil conditions but the heaviest clays, drainage can be carried out either by laying tiles or digging open ditches. If the ground is pure peat, tiles are not very satisfactory. But if the soil is a heavy clay or is limy, it is essential to make raised beds. These are now used very successfully in many parts of the United States of America. There, either a 100% new soil mixture is added above the existing soil level and held in position by boards, or about 30% of the top soil is added to organic materials and very well incorporated into

17

a more friable mixture. Coarse sawdust is ideal, mixed with a nitrogen fertilizer to aid rotting and to avoid nitrogen starvation of the plants, but in Britain this type of sawdust is rarely available. A combination of all or some of the following should give good results: sandy soil, oak or beech leaf-mould, spruce or pine needles, forest litter, wood chips, shredded bark, rotten wood, bracken litter, hop manure and fibrous or coarse peat moss. Sawdust and shredded bark should have ammonium sulphate added, at the rate of 12 lb per 1000 sq.ft (5.5 kg per 93 m²) for every inch (2.5 cm) applied.

For individual holes, the quantity of peat (bagged or baled, moss or fibrous) and leaf-mould to be added depends on the amount of organic matter already present in the soil. Where organic matter is lacking, fork over the base of the hole, then add at least two large full shovels each of peat and leaf-mould and mix well in. Break up the edge of the hole where it meets the hard ground so as not to leave a sudden division between made up ground and undug soil.

Similarly, beds lacking in organic matter should have at least three inches (8 cm) of peat and leaf-mould spread on them and this should be very well forked in with any clods broken up. Although almost any peat is better than none, ideally coarse fibrous peat is best, either sedge or sphagnum. The leaf-mould should be beech or oak or a combination of the two, only from trees grown on acid soil. It had been proved that leaf-mould collected from chalk or limy areas is alkaline and therefore unsuitable for rhododendrons.

For alpine varieties, peat beds are ideal, built up on terraces made with peat blocks. The blocks should be as large and even as possible and they are better set in position when they are damp, as when really dry they take a long time to swell and then distort the line of the wall. Soak them if necessary. The walls are better when not more than three or four blocks high, laid like bricks, but slanted inwards and well packed with soil both behind and under the blocks. Wire pegs help to keep them in place. Prepare the actual beds as described above. A few small plants can be inserted in the wall, between the blocks.

Only large growing rhododendrons should be planted in individual holes. All azaleas and dwarf rhododendrons appreciate beds much better and will be kept free of weeds more easily.

IN THE GREENHOUSE AND IN THE HOUSE

Many different rhododendrons and azaleas may be grown indoors, either in pots or in other containers which can be brought into the house, or planted in beds in the greenhouse. Most of those are grown indoors because they are tender, but certain hardy evergreen azaleas do well inside and now certain hybrid rhododendrons are being forced by combinations of specially regulated day-lengths and chemical growth controllers.

The ordinary indoor azaleas are nearly all grown in Belgium and exported from there and from Holland to Britain to force into flower during the winter. If well looked after, that is, repotted and properly watered and fed, there is no reason why these azaleas should not last for years and grow into fine specimens. For those with no greenhouse, keep them well watered until flowering has finished and then repot, using a good coarse soilless compost. John Innes potting mixture would be too far removed from the original peat and the plant will have difficulty rooting into a mixture different to that to which it was accustomed. Use the recommended fertilizers without chalk; tableted fertilizers are the simplest to apply. Never allow the root ball to dry out at any time.

Many of the scented rhododendrons do well indoors. Nearly all are too tender to survive outside in any but the mildest coastal areas. The flowers are white tinged with pink and some have the most delicious scent, a joy in the house in the early spring.

Another group that is excellent indoors are the early species, such as R. leucaspis and R. moupinense and hybrids like 'Cilpinense', often growing a better shape than the scented varieties. These are mostly pink, yellow or white and free flowering from February to March with very little forcing. In fact if they are forced too much, some flower colour and size is lost.

During the summer, all these varieties in pots, including the azaleas, should be plunged in soil or ashes outside after the danger of frost is over, in a relatively shady position, say at the foot of a north-facing wall or hedge. Keep well watered in dry weather and bring indoors again in autumn before any frost occurs. If there is no greenhouse, place by a window in a coolish room and again remember to keep damp. If there is a greenhouse but no heat, plunge the pots up to the rims and keep well ventilated in all but cold frosty weather. If some heat is possible, set the temperature at 40°F (4.5°C) or lower until at least February, when the buds start swelling and the heat can be raised a little. Some azaleas, if given extra heat, will open for Christmas. Keep the house well ventilated unless the weather is cold. Many of these plants are likely to drop their buds if the temperature goes too high or the pots dry out. Naturally, severe frost will damage the buds of the more tender varieties and all are susceptible once the buds begin to swell. In spring and early summer, keep the greenhouse well damped down in sunny weather.

Rhododendron luteum (p.60), the well known yellow azalea, has fragrant flowers

Many potted azaleas or rhododendrons may become leggy or spread too much. Unfortunately most of the scented kinds are inclined to sprawl and produce few branches. Pinching out the growth buds may induce more branching, or the longest shoots may be cut back to where there is a bud or shorter growth. 'Fragrantissimum', a pure white, large flowered, scented rhododendron, is sometimes tied in all round to produce a 'basket' effect.

In the greenhouse, beds should have at least 1 foot (30 cm) of soil with perfect drainage underneath. An ideal mixture is equal parts of sandy acid loam, peat and oak or beech leaf-mould and/or half-rotted conifer needles.

Another use for the greenhouse or frames is for dwarf rhododendrons, either for the show bench, to protect plants from atmospheric pollution or when avoiding alkaline soil. They may be grown indoors throughout the year. Square wooden boxes dry out less than pots and can be recommended. Leave a space at the top of the pot or box of $1\frac{1}{2}$ to 2 inches (4 to 5 cm) to allow for a top dressing, and repot them every two years. Cut back if necessary immediately after flowering. Either soilless or John Innes potting compost may be used, without chalk, possibly with the addition of oak or beech leaf-mould. If the water is a little hard, add $\frac{1}{2}$ oz of ferrous sulphate per gallon (14 g per 4.5 litres), but if very hard, use only rain water.

Where and how to plant

WHAT TIME OF YEAR

One of the excellent characters of rhododendrons, including azaleas, is that they are easy to move, even when quite large, providing they can be man-handled.

It is possible to move rhododendrons throughout the year. But anything transplanted in late spring and summer will need extra care over watering and shading. One advantage of moving a plant in flower is that a colour scheme can be arranged while it can be seen what is wanted.

Early autumn is the ideal time to plant. The roots get a chance to settle in before winter and then the winter snow and rains bed the plant in thoroughly before spring. Late autumn planting is quite satisfactory and so is planting in early spring, but the danger in spring is the dry east wind which can desiccate a plant before it is established, so care should be taken over extra watering and shelter. Do not plant into frozen ground.

One disadvantage often overlooked comes with buying rhododendrons from a nursery in an earlier locality then one's own. Even in Scotland, there may be at least two weeks' difference between a low sheltered garden facing south and a cold exposed garden at 1000 ft (300 m) above sea level. A plant transferred from the low area to the high, in spring, could be a full two weeks ahead of what it would have been had it been transferred in the autumn, making it far more suspectible to a cold spring spell.

Garden centres are now found all over the country and a higher and higher proportion of plants are being sold from these, in particular plants in some type of container when in flower, for planting direct into the garden. This is an excellent idea because one knows exactly what is being bought, but such plants often take longer to become established and will need more care over watering for the rest of their first season. Loosen the root ball if a plant is pot bound.

Do not be surprised if a well-budded specimen does not flower again for a year or two. Several nurserymen prepare their plants to be well budded the year they are sold and then the plants take a year or two to recover and grow away again. Many of the larger varieties are better bought without flower buds. It is far better to sacrifice flowers at an early age for growth, and thus end up with a much finer specimen plant.

With modern methods of rooting cuttings, it should no longer be necessary to propagate by grafting, except for a few difficult varieties. So many rhododendrons grafted on to R. *ponticum* are ultimately overgrown by the rootstock taking over. If grafting is really necessary, it should be done on either species or cultivars that do not sucker readily.

Many species are hard to propagate from cuttings and are uneconomic to layer. Named clonal selections of these species are often very hard to find and are expensive. By hand pollinating, using two good forms of a species, relatively cheap seedlings may be produced in quantity and these are excellent value, nearly all proving as good if not better than their parents. Wild collected seed is now more readily available again from China. It is great fun to grow plants from wild seed, especially if it is known exactly from where they originated and they may prove to be special forms or even new species.

For those people who want instant rhododendrons, large plants can be bought but they are relatively expensive and do not always make such fine specimens as those grown on from the normal size available. These plants generally have to have quite a proportion of their root system and/or the soil ball removed for transport, and therefore require considerable care for the first year or two, before becoming established.

HOW TO PLANT CORRECTLY

Never plant a rhododendron too deeply. Only a bare sprinkling of soil should be put on top of the root ball and it is usually simple to find the mark of the old soil-level near the base of the stem. Space out any loose roots at their proper level and push soil gently underneath them. The one exception to this method is with young grafted plants. These should be placed a little deeper each time they are moved so that the scion (above the graft union) can form roots itself. Never mound up soil around the stem after planting. Never tramp in too firmly, especially in heavy soil, because rhododendrons like well aerated soil conditions. It is most important to water in well after planting with a hose or coarse rose on a watering can.

It is sometimes necessary to firm a rather top-heavy plant around the neck, but staking is usually needed as well. If possible, push or knock in the stake before planting and tie securely with fibre string or raffia, not wire or plastic string which may eat into the stem if left on too long.

On a very light, well drained soil, especially on a slope, planting in a 'saucer' is beneficial. Not only does it conserve moisture, but also leaves a place to hold a mulch. Never plant on a mound when the soil is liable to dry out. Only where the rainfall is very heavy or the drainage imperfect are mounds advisable.

The distance to plant is a matter of choice, whether close, where an immediate effect is desired, or further apart, when a few years

The normal correct planting level for rhododendrons.

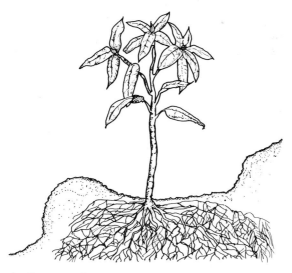

Saucer planting on a slope.

23

may be taken to close the gaps. Dwarfs and evergreen azaleas are relatively small and can easily be transplanted when they become crowded, but the larger varieties can be more difficult owing to their size and the weight of the root ball. It is always better to give too much, rather than too little room. Really well spaced out bushes, with branches down to ground level and enough space to walk round them, are infinitely preferable to lanky overcrowded specimens reaching for the sky, where one strains one's neck to see the flowers! Of course it takes a long time to reach this state of affairs, but do look to the future when planting. A good idea is to plant three or more of one variety close together, especially with dwarfs, as rhododendrons are naturally communal plants.

Mound planting for a wet site.

Regular care

MULCHES

A mulch is a layer of organic matter applied to the surface of the soil. It serves various purposes: (1) To retain moisture. (2) To control weeds. (3) To provide organic matter as a nutrient. (4) To modify the surface temperature of the soil. (5) To prevent erosion by rain. (6) To reduce the depth to which frost reaches in the ground. In climates with hot summers and cold winters, all these points are of importance, but in Britain, (1), (2) and (3) are of the most significance.

Good mulches to use here are oak and beech leaf-mould, pine and spruce needles, chopped or pulverised fresh bracken fronds, wood or bark chips and pulverised bark. Hop manure is another alternative. Sawdust is only really good if coarse; few saws used in this country produce this grade, because the teeth are not large enough. Fine sawdust tends to mat down too much and form a cake, although all sawdust is excellent if completely rotted before use. Micro-organisms take nitrogen from the soil for the breakdown of wood by-products, robbing the plants of nitrogen underneath. Therefore extra nitrogen must be added as ammonium sulphate. This should be applied at approximately 12 lb per 1000 sq.ft (5.5 kg per 93 m²) of surface for every inch (2.5 cm) depth of sawdust put on. Some gardeners give several light applications of fertilizer instead of one heavy one. Excellent partially decomposed shredded bark is now available which does not require added nitrogen.

Rough peat is a good mulch but dries out too much in hot, dry weather and then becomes difficult to wet properly again. It also tends to encourage too many surface roots, which are easily damaged by drought and frost.

Really unsuitable mulches are grass cuttings which become a horrid, soggy mat and may heat and kill the roots underneath; and leaf-mould either from alkaline soil or from such trees as elm, sycamore, lime and horse chestnut. These break down to give an alkaline reaction and have a powdery texture, both being undesirable for rhododendrons. Straw and hay are messy, liable to blow away and hay seeds add to the weeds.

To be successful for suppressing weeds and conserving moisture, a mulch should be at least 3 inches (7.5 cm) deep. The easiest way to supply a rhododendron with a mulch of leaves is to put any prunings of dead wood, fallen branches or twigs around the root area of big, established bushes. This may be considered a little unsightly by some people. All large branches can be cut or broken into smaller bits. These trap the leaves when they fall where they are wanted over the rhododendron roots, instead of being blown away. Never collect and burn leaves among these plants, except when large leaves have collected on top of dwarfs where they can rot the foliage underneath.

FEEDING

Various concentrated fertilizers, both organic and inorganic, can be used on the majority of rhododendrons in *moderation*, but they are no substitute for organic matter. If a compound of ready mixed fertilizer is used, it should contain a relatively small amount of nitrogen, in ammonium form if possible. Most fertilizers are sold with an analysis giving the nitrogen, phosphorus and potassium content, using the abbreviations, N.P.K. For use in the spring, a mixture of 12N, 6P, 6K is ideal applied at 1 oz per sq.yd (33 g per m²).

Rhododendrons and azaleas that are happy, that is, have healthy foliage, adequate growth and when mature enough, flower freely, should not be given fertilizers and manures. With an abundance of good leaf mould and a suitable soil underneath, plants rarely need extra feeding. But in many cases, especially on light peaty or hungry soils, these materials can be beneficial.

The varieties that respond best to added fertilizer are the deciduous hybrid azaleas of the Exbury, Mollis and Ghent types, also some of the so-called hardy hybrid rhododendrons such as 'Pink Pearl' and 'Purple Splendour'. Many others, especially those related to *R. neriiflorum* and *R. taliense*, are susceptible to doses of nitrogen and get leaf scorch very easily.

Nitrogen is of value for inducing growth and healthy foliage. Phosphate and potassium help the ripening of wood and the formation of flower buds. Many other elements are also essential for the well-being of a plant; for example magnesium for photosynthesis (formation of chlorophyll in the leaf) and sulphur and calcium in small quantities are also necessary. The trace elements, likewise, must be available. Luckily all are usually present in the average soil in sufficient quantities, but if not there are various compound fertilizers and liquid feeds which now contain all the elements.

Several slow-acting compounds now available are excellent for trees and shrubs. In very small quantities, organic manures, such as bone meal, hoof and horn, and fish meal are suitable. Bone meal contains a minute amount of lime, but this is so small it does not harm rhododendrons.

Beware of all farmyard manures. Any used should be really well rotted. Cow manure is sometimes used, but is not as good as leaf-mould or needles. Hen manure has led to disasters from excess ammonia. The golden rule is, always use fertilizers and manures in moderation and follow instructions carefully. Better to be safe than sorry.

LIME

Much has been written on the subject of limy and chalky soils in relation to rhododendrons. If excess calcium is present in the soil, rhododendrons take up too much of it and poison themselves. Soils in which they grow naturally are low in calcium and rhododendrons are very efficient in utilising any that is available.

The whole question of soils and the elements contained therein is very complex, and cannot be explained here. Not only are rhododendrons poisoned by lime, but excessive quantities lock up other elements present in such a way that the plants cannot use them. The result is usually severe chlorosis and frequently death. There is no easy way of growing rhododendrons on lime or chalk soils. Raised beds have been mentioned on pp.17–18. Another suggestion is to line holes with flowers of sulphur and fill with rotted bracken and acid peat which are also mixed with the soil at the edge of the hole. Then mulch with pine needles and chopped bracken, every year. Some rhododendrons have grown well this way for years.

Various chemical compounds are available for helping rhododendrons to grow in unsuitable soils: these are chelates and fritted trace elements. While they are of some value in improving the colour of foliage and the general health of rhododendrons, the former is liable to cause severe scorch and death even if the instructions are carried out carefully. These chemicals make the various trace elements, such as iron and manganese, available to the plants. It is said that rhododendrons are more easily grown on limestone than on pure chalk. See pp.47–54 for the most lime tolerant species.

WATERING

Many sheltered woodland gardens with a heavy rainfall and a soil rich in organic matter rarely, if ever, really suffer from drought, once rhododendrons are fully established. But many of us are not so lucky. Where soil dries out quickly, a dry period of a month or more can cause severe stress. If one of these droughts occurs during the main growing season from April to July, it can be serious, and if no watering is done, plants can suffer, especially in the first season or two after planting. Plants which have been well mulched are less susceptible to drought, because the layer of organic matter on the soil surface prevents some loss of water.

In a large garden there are always certain areas which dry out first. This may be because of too much sun, shallow soil, overhead trees or tree roots. Any bush in full growth will need special attention at these times.

When watering always give a really good soak. Various modern overhead sprinklers are now on the market, mostly reliable, and many do not require much pressure; an alternative is the various types of seep hose. A sprinkler can be left on for at least 3 hours, but soil conditions and the type of equipment used must be considered when deciding the length of time to water. The snag comes during the rare, really prolonged drought which may last for several months and when the use of a hose is prohibited.

If the water is strongly alkaline, it should not of course be used, and rain water is unlikely to be available in sufficient quantities for continual use outdoors. Do not use water softened artificially. Be cautious over using water with detergents in it. Bath water with soap is preferable.

Watering is best done in the early morning so as to soak in before the sun rises, and although no harm has been noticed by watering during strong sunlight at mid-day, there must be some evaporation.

WEEDKILLERS AND CULTIVATION

It is only in the last few years that really suitable reliably safe weedkillers have come on the market. Before using herbicides all of the makers' instructions must be read very carefully. Avoid using a fine spray in windy weather so that drifting spray does not damage plants nearby.

Rhododendrons and azaleas hate grass and other weeds growing on top of their shallow root system. With a knapsack sprayer or a watering can, it is easy to treat ground around established bushes.

Weedkillers can be divided into several groups. There are total

Opposite above: 'Klondyke' (p.62), an example of the Exbury hybrid azaleas
Below: *Rhododendron thomsonii* (p.48) has a smooth peeling bark and fine foliage

weedkillers: sodium chlorate is the best known and a good alternative is glyphosate; both should be used at least six months before planting anything in the treated area. Simazine and relations are also total weedkillers of a kind, when used at high concentrations. Applied at lower concentrations, they are very good for killing germinating weed seeds in otherwise clean ground, but they are very persistent in the soil. They are also excellent on paths. The 2,4-D, mecoprop and dicamba mixture is very good against broadleaved herbaceous weeds, especially nettles. It is best applied in late spring. Most woody weeds grow again after the first application. Certain brands of weedkiller are rather volatile and give off fumes which can cause distortion in nearby young growth. To avoid distortion, cut down weeds in spring and spray re-growth in early autumn.

Paraquat with diquat is highly effective for burning off top growth of most weeds and is broken down in the soil immediately, except on peat and other pure organic matter. It is safe to use right up to the trunks of rhododendrons, but any drop which gets onto the foliage will cause a brown spot and it will damage green wood. It is relatively ineffective on nettles but severely checks bishop's weed (*Aegopodium podagraria*); mosses are encouraged. It will be found necessary to apply it two or three times during the season for complete control of annual weeds.

As a general rule, the soil around rhododendrons should *not* be cultivated, because of their shallow root system. A careful shallow hoeing in dry weather does little harm, provided there are no roots on the surface. Deeper hoeing and digging or forking can damage the roots severely.

Rhododendrons appreciate loose, well aerated soil, as already stated. To keep carefully prepared beds and holes in good condition, avoid walking on them as much as possible. Regular paths should never cross within the area of roots (root area is roughly similar to the branch spread) and beds should either be made narrow enough to reach from each side or have stepping stones strategically placed for walking on.

PRUNING

Rhododendrons do not need regular pruning; only in special circumstances is any pruning necessary. Specimens retrieved from old collections are often lanky and drawn and in most cases respond well to cutting back. The chief exceptions are varieties with smooth bark, many of the big-leaved species, and R. *thomsonii*, R. *taliense* and their relatives. If pruning is necessary, it is generally better to cut back a portion at a time so that as many green leaves are left as possible. Certain varieties which grow away well, such as many hardy hybrids (especially those containing R. *ponticum* blood), R. *triflorum*, R. *lapponicum* and their relatives and deciduous azaleas, can break well from old wood. Even with them, it is safer not to be too drastic all at once. Try to cut just above dormant buds. Grafted plants may require regular inspection for *ponticum* suckers, which should be wrenched off at the base, not cut.

Some dwarfs, notably R. *lapponicum* and its allies, can stand an occasional pruning with shears.

Cutting back is best done in the early spring or after flowering. Sometimes a little shaping can be done by cutting branches for indoor decoration. Always cut right back to a trunk or live shoot, for dead stumps only encourage disease. It is seldom practical to reduce the overall dimension of a rhododendron by pruning. Usually the result is a ruined bush.

All rhododendrons look so much healthier if all dead wood is cut out. When doing this job, many half dead branches can also be removed.

DEAD-HEADING

There is no doubt that the careful removal of dead rhododendron flowers, just after flowering, is beneficial to the plant and also promotes the formation of flower buds for the following year. Not only are dead seed heads often unsightly, but the production of seed in large quantities uses a considerable amount of the plant's energy.

It is simply not possible for most people to dead-head all their rhododendrons. Generally, those in most need of being done are the large-leaved species, which can form gigantic capsules. Certain dwarfs, such as R. *campylogynum*, have long flower stalks and the seed capsules are set up well above the leaves. These can be removed quickly with a small pair of scissors. The removal of the large flower heads can be speedily done by hand, once the knack is learned. Small trusses can be snapped off between finger and thumb. The largest varieties are better done with two hands as some force is needed and it is too easy to break off the whole shoot. Sometimes the trusses come away cleanly just above the topmost leaves, but in others it is just as well to knock off the individual spent flowers. Be careful not to knock off young shoots starting to grow.

It is always worthwhile dead-heading newly planted specimens and of course any plants that appear to lack vigour or are not thriving.

Propagation

Propagation can be divided into two completely separate sections. One is vegetative propagation, which means taking some part of an existing plant and making it into another plant, either by a cutting, layer or graft. Only in this way can something exactly similar to the original be produced. The other method is by seed. Even when the seed breeds true and is not deliberately or accidentally hybridised, it will not give the exact replica of its parent. Therefore, hybrids and special clones should always be propagated vegetatively and only species and deliberate new crosses should be raised from seed.

VEGETATIVE PROPAGATION

Cuttings

Great advances have been made in recent years in the art of rooting cuttings, and we now have the help of polythene, hormone rooting powders and automatic mist sprays. For the beginner wishing to grow just a handful of young plants, polythene is perhaps the greatest boon. Various propagation units are readily available such as trays with clear Perspex lids, and some with electric heating. Even small mist units can be bought. These consist of an electric unit with overhead nozzles from which a fine spray is emitted; this is automatically controlled according to the sunlight. The greater the amount of sunshine the more frequent are the bursts of mist.

The two main points to remember when attempting to root any rhododendron cuttings are that the foliage must never be allowed to wilt and that the drainage in the rooting medium must be perfect. Any more or less airtight container, which does not receive the direct sun and yet lets in the maximum light, will prove suitable for the easier varieties. Outdoor frames at the back of a north wall are excellent and, on a smaller scale, pots or boxes enclosed in a polythene bag and kept airtight can be successful. Any container used should be scrupulously clean. The best rooting medium is a 50/50 mixture of finest quality sphagnum peat and sharp sand or fine gravel or a 50/50 peat/pulverised pine bark mixture. Whatever type of container is used, ensure excellent drainage at the bottom. The rooting medium should be

A cutting showing slicing on both sides of the base of the cutting as an aid to rooting

about 3 inches (7.5 cm) deep and must be renewed with each batch of cuttings.

The easiest cuttings to root and grow are evergreen azaleas, and some dwarf rhododendrons such as R. *impeditum* and 'Elizabeth'. A few of the bigger hybrids are not too difficult.

Nearly all cuttings should be taken in a half ripe condition, which means a cutting which will bend but not break until bent double. Most are ready in July and August, with a few not ripe enough until September. If taken too soft, the cuttings will rot and if too hard, they take much longer to root, if they root at all.

Cuttings of the dwarf alpine varieties and evergreen azaleas should not be over 2 inches (5 cm) long and can be less. Larger varieties should be less than 4 inches (10 cm) long. Always use a sharp knife and cut cleanly through the wood. Only young growth should be used and there is no need to leave a heel of old wood, but if possible, cut at a node, trimming off the lower leaves. With some cultivars that are more difficult to root, slicing down each side of the base of the cutting may help to stimulate rooting. Most cuttings can be pushed into the rooting medium, which should not be firmed. Water in well.

Proprietary hormones can be used and are generally of some benefit. In a greenhouse, many cuttings will root in about three to four months. These can be put out into a cold frame after having been hardened off. Many cuttings are lost after they have rooted during the period of acclimatisation before planting out, and this

33

must be done gradually. Another aid to rooting with more difficult cuttings is 'bottom heat', when the rooting medium is heated at about 60–70°F (15–21°C) by thermostatically controlled electric cables laid at least 3 inches (7.5 cm) below surface.

Potting soil

Any potting compost without chalk will suffice, but it should be loose and friable. If loam is used it must be of a light sandy nature. A good mixture is one quarter peat (preferably sphagnum and not too dusty), a quarter pulverised pine bark, a quarter oak or/and beech leaf-mould or half rotted conifer needles and a quarter washed coarse sand or fine gravel. Fertilizers may be added to speed up growth at the rate of 1 oz (28 g) superphosphate, $\frac{1}{2}$ oz (14 g) potassium sulphate, $\frac{1}{2}$ oz ammonium sulphate and $\frac{1}{2}$ oz magnesium sulphate (Epsom salts) per bushel (36 litres).

When potting or boxing rooted cuttings, firm very lightly. A liquid foliar feed may be applied once a fortnight but stop this if any scorching of the leaves occurs. Do not apply after July.

Layering

This is perhaps the simplest method of propagation, and can be used for all varieties. Layering means placing a branch in soil while it is still attached to the parent plant and leaving it there until it is well rooted. This may take from one to three or even

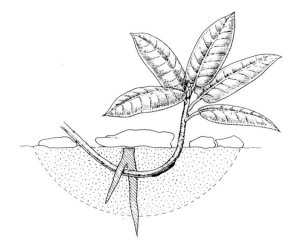

Layering: the branch is held in place by a peg, covered with stones

more years. Layering can be done where just one or more low branches are pegged down, or where a whole plant is layered, using every shoot possible. In the latter case, the root ball is often put on its side to ease the bending down of the branches. This method is occasionally used in nurseries.

The simplest way to layer is to select a low branch near the ground, and then dig out a little trench underneath it which should be filled with peat or a mixture of peat, sand and leaf-mould. Bend the branch at the tip into as upright a position as possible and hold it like this with a stake and some string. In an open or dry situation, do not mound up the soil over the branch. Only use relatively young shoots. Older ones will not bend easily, will take longer to root and will prove harder to establish, once removed from the parent.

In damp shady places, an excellent alternative to this method is to root into a box filled with a similar mixture. With this method the roots of the parent plant are not disturbed, it is often possible to use a branch at a higher level, and moving the layer after rooting is much easier. Flat stones may be placed on top of the branches, partly to hold them in position, and partly to retain moisture around the area of rooting. By bending up the shoot the root plant has a better shape and it also helps to speed up rooting. Slitting the stem at the bend can further stimulate the rooting.

When a good mat of roots has formed (which may take at least two years), sever the branch just behind the roots and lift carefully to keep the roots intact. Make sure the roots are damp before moving. It is best to establish new layers in a shady nursery bed before planting out into the final position. Leggy specimens of dwarfs can be pegged down all round the perimeter and likewise bent into an upright posture by using stones.

The great disadvantage of ground layering is that many specimens have no branches in reach of the soil. Air layering can be tried instead. This is done by wrapping sphagnum moss around a youngish shoot and encasing this in polythene, securely taping each end. One problem with this method is to stop water running down the stem and making the moss too wet for rooting. Air layering usually takes even longer than the first method and the severed layer is quite hard to establish.

Grafting

There are many different ways of grafting, but for rhododendrons the simplest is a saddle graft. Grafting should be done only after all other methods of propagation have failed, i.e. if layering is impossible and cuttings next to impossible to root.

Grafting can be done at various times of the year, but the best time is in mid-winter to March. Only vigorous young seedlings and/or rooted cuttings should be used as rootstocks, with a stem roughly equal to the thickness of the scion to be grafted. This should average about pencil thickness.

The best stocks have single stems. These can be established in pots or plunged in peat and bark in a frame. *Rhododendron ponticum* is the easiest stock to acquire and to work with, but its habit of producing suckers should rule out its use altogether. Seedlings of R. *decorum* and R. *fortunei* are as good as any, or use rooted cuttings of 'Cunningham's White' or the thinner 'Elizabeth'. For big-leaved species, any similar seedling stock will suffice.

When preparing the rootstock, remove any side shoots, buds or leaves low down, so as to leave a clean stem for a few inches above soil level. Select only strong, healthy shoots for the scions. Cut a slice up each side of the stem of the rootstock, with a sharp clean knife, for one to two inches (2.5 to 5 cm) to leave a wedge shape. Split the base of the scion to a similar distance up the stem; push the scion gently on to the wedge of severed stock and see that the bark coincides on one side at least. Bind tightly with a tape of polythene, a large rubber band cut open or raffia, dust with

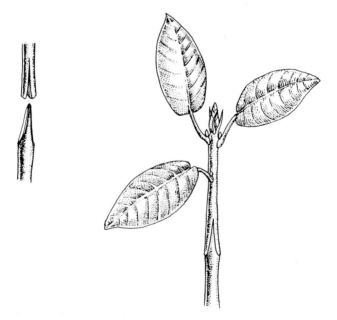

Saddle grafting: the graft union (right) is shown before binding: left, the wedge-shaped rootstock is shown below

captan (or equivalent fungicide) and place in an airtight frame or in a polythene bag, with two wire hoops to keep the bag off the foliage, and tie the top tightly. Shade from direct sunlight. If overwatered, the stock may die. For best results apply a gentle heat, not over 60°F (15°C). If the scion wilts, it invariably dies. Harden off slowly over a period of several weeks, gradually allowing a little more air every few days. To overwinter, place in a shady position in the open or in a frame.

PROPAGATION BY SEED

All rhododendron and azalea seed is small and light. It ripens from August to January, but most capsules turn brown from October to December and must be watched carefully or much of the seed may be shed. Any seed collected at random in a collection of mixed varieties is liable to have been pollinated by bees, and so be of mixed parentage. The only way to be sure that a species will come true to type is to hand pollinate. This is simply done by first removing petals and stamens from a nearly open flower, being careful not to damage the pistil which is in the middle. Label carefully and two or three days later, apply pollen from the stamens, if possible off another plant of the same species,

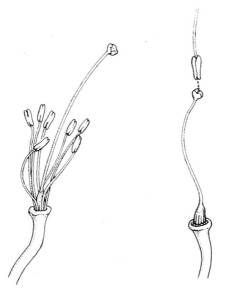

Preparing a flower for pollination; left: the corolla removed, right: the stamens removed leaving the pistil to be pollinated

or if hybridising, from the intended male parent. Many rhododendrons are infertile with their own pollen.

After collection, the seed capsules should be dried carefully in an open container, taking care not to overheat. When the capsules split open, carefully shake out the seed and pick out bits of capsule or other foreign matter as these encourage mould on the seed pan after sowing.

The seed can be stored in little envelopes in a closed tin for several months. Stored in airtight jars in a household refrigerator, the seed will keep for several years. Vireya species and hybrids must be sown as soon as the seeds are ripe.

Sow on finely sifted peat or, for very special seeds, on riddled live sphagnum – no mould will occur on this. Place peat or sphagnum in clean pans or boxes, firm and level out carefully. Always soak the medium from underneath in soft water before sowing. Sow the seed thinly, especially the very small seed of dwarfs, and do not cover. Label, giving name, origin and date sown. Sowing may be done in January if heat is available or postponed until March. Dwarf lepidotes are best germinated and grown on without heat in a cold frame. Sow in January–February; frost will do no harm before they germinate. Cover pans or boxes preferably with perforated polythene or, if unobtainable, with clean glass plus newspaper. The glass needs to be turned daily. No further watering should be necessary until well after germination which begins two to three weeks later. If glass is used, it can soon be removed.

The young seedlings must never be allowed to dry out and may be shaded by one layer of paper to keep off direct sunlight, Occasional watering should be done from below by standing the pan or box in water, letting the water soak in gradually until the surface is moist. Occasional syringing can be done from above but watch out for mould caused by excess dampness on the leaves; apply the fungicide captan or equivalent if necessary. Transplant into boxes or frames when big enough to handle. If sown thinly, this pricking out can be delayed until the following spring but growth will be slower. Use the same compost for pricking out as for rooted cuttings. Well diluted liquid feed may be applied every second week of the growing season.

Another method of raising seedlings, which takes less looking after at the early stages, is to use clear plastic food containers with air-tight lids. Fill the container to within an inch of the top, level out carefully and water and sow the seeds as before. When the first true leaves have appeared after the two cotyledons, gradually take off the lid for short periods during the day over a week or two. Thereafter treat as before.

Pests and diseases

PESTS

Although rhododendrons in general are relatively free from attacks by pests, there are a few that can occasionally cause serious damage.

Aphids

Aphids often attack the young growth of rhododendrons, especially any late growth chiefly on hybrids in a dry season. These sap sucking insects cause leaves to become curled and distorted. In severe cases, spray with pirimicarb, pirimiphos-methyl or a systemic insecticide.

Caterpillars

Usually not serious but can disfigure foliage, especially in woodland. Light infestations can be picked off by hand. When young leaves are being badly eaten, spray with insecticides such as HCH, pirimiphos-methyl or permethrin. Whole sections are eaten as opposed to just notches with weevils (see below).

Rhododendron lacebug

Adults and nymphs of this small ($\frac{3}{16}$ in.; 4 mm) brownish black insect with lace-like wings suck sap from May onwards on leaf undersides. They cause a fine yellowish mottling of the leaf upper surface and a sticky rusty brown discoloration below. Worst in sunny positions. Spray leaf undersides with HCH, malathion or dimethoate early and late June.

Rhododendron leafhopper

Only of importance because it can spread bud blast. The hopper can be controlled where bud blast is really troublesome by spraying at 10 to 14 day intervals as necessary from early August onwards with HCH, fenitrothion, permethrin or dimethoate.

Vine weevils

These slow moving dull black beetles are active at night during the summer months. They create irregular notches on leaf margins. The larvae, white with light brown heads, feed on roots and stems below and around soil level. Established plants are rarely severely damaged but young plants, especially those in containers may be killed by the larvae. In bad cases, the adults may be controlled by spraying the soil surface and foliage with HCH or fenitrothion at dusk. The young larvae can be controlled by drenching the soil with permethrin in August (I find HCH can severely damage young camellias if given as a soil drench).

Whitefly

Evergreen azaleas are particulary susceptible to these. The tiny white moth-like insects and their nymphs suck sap on the leaf undersides, mostly in June and July. They can cause yellowing of the foliage plus sooty mould from their excreted honeydew. Spray the leaf undersides with permethrin, repeating several times if the attack is severe.

Mammals

These are much more damaging. Rabbits, roe and other deer, hares and sheep are fond of many varieties, especially when young and newly planted. Those most liable to be attacked are all azaleas and many dwarf rhododendrons. If serious, wire or plastic netting is the only practical answer, other than destroying the culprits. Either the whole garden can be enclosed or individual susceptible specimens can be protected. Rabbits are only likely to be really troublesome if plentiful. They occasionally bark young rhododendrons, so the stems may need protection. Dogs' (as opposed to bitches') urine burns nasty holes in dwarf varieties and can even prove fatal. Moles loosen the soil and even throw young plants out of the soil. They are best trapped in their runs.

Birds

Blackbirds pull out small plants – nets are the only answer. Tits ruin flowers, particularly red ones, by pecking for nectar. Feeding with nuts and fat helps to keep the birds otherwise occupied!
  Do keep human visitors from walking all over your beds!

DISEASES

A few diseases have become more widespread in recent years, especially powdery mildew and honey fungus from elm stumps.

Powdery mildew

A relatively new type of this disease has become quite serious and has now spread all over the country. A faint whitish powder coats parts of the leaf undersurface associated with discoloured patches on both sides. Severe cases can lead to defoliation. The symptoms usually first appear in August and become progresively worse, until diseased leaves fall in early spring. It is particularly bad after a prolonged wet spell in late summer or autumn. Rhododendron cinnabarinum and its hybrids are particularly susceptible, as are hybrids with Fortunea and Campylocarpa blood. Hybrids of moupinense and some others are also showing susceptibility. Spray monthly from spring to autumn and during mild spells in winter, thoroughly wetting both leaf surfaces, using benomyl, bupirimate with triforine, or carbendazim mixtures, alternating these to give the best control.

Honey fungus

Caused by Armillaria species, this is a disease liable to strike anywhere. It normally lives on dead, woody tissue, but unfortunately it often attacks live plants as well. Those most susceptible are plants newly transplanted, which have been damaged by wind shake, water-logging, or some other mechanical injury, usually at or below soil level. Some shrubs die off branch by branch, while others may suddenly collapse shortly after showing unhealthy foliage symptoms. Long brown or black boot-lace-like strands may run through the soil, usually coming from rotting tree stumps and these start the infection. Honey-coloured fructifications may also appear in the autumn.

Removal of all old stumps and dead rhododendrons should help to reduce the spread of the disease, but a possible cure is a proprietary phenolic fungicide. This can be used to sterilize infected soil and on tree stumps left in the ground. It is not, however, recommended for direct use on fibrous-rooted plants such as rhododendrons.

Leaf spots

These black or brown spots on the leaves usually occur on badly drained or overshaded bushes, especially in a wet season. They are not serious except that they do show that the growing conditions could be improved. If the trouble persists spray with benomyl, carbendazim, thiophanate-methyl or mancozeb, after flowering, repeating twice at 10– to 14–day intervals.

Petal blight

This is a comparatively rare disease in Britain and attacks the flowers of evergreen azaleas and other rhododendrons. It starts in damp weather as little brown spots on the flowers. These grow rapidly, turning the whole flower into pulp which sticks on the branches and remains very unsightly. Avoid overhead watering when the plants are in flower. If trouble is suspected, spray with mancozeb or benomyl two or three times a flowering season.

Bud blast

This is not to be confused with frost damage. The flower buds die and little black spore-producing bristles cover the buds, which are not present when frosted. Certain varieties are most susceptible, notably R. *ponticum* and R. *caucasicum* and their hybrids. It is probably spread by the rhododendron leafhopper. Collect and burn affected buds.

Galls

These are common on evergreen azaleas and R. *ferrugineum*, R. *hirsutum*, R. *myrtifolium* and their hybrids. They appear as ugly green, pink or red swellings on the leaves, stems or flowers and later turn white when sporing. Hand pick and burn, or spray with bordeaux mixture or other copper fungicide or mancozeb as the new leaves appear.

Lichen

This is not a disease, rather a disfigurement. It is very common, especially on azaleas in wet areas, more so on those which are lacking in vigour. Liberal top dressing (see p.26), applications of a foliar feed and cutting out old wood may help.

OTHER EVILS

Bark split

This injury is caused by early autumn or late spring frosts when the sap is running. Young growth is nearly always killed at the same time. The splitting of the bark can occur anywhere from ground level up to one-year-old shoots. Prevention is perhaps more reliable than a cure. Protection of the base of the stem may be achieved by wrapping it with fibreglass, polystyrene, old sacks or hessian, or mounding up sawdust, pine needles, soil etc.

The beautiful yellow-flowered *Rhododendron campylocarpum* (p.48)

Remember to remove these once the dangers of frost are over. This type of trouble usually takes place after a very early spring brings on young growth followed by a hard frost.

Secondary young growth usually comes away if the first flush is frosted, but it is never so robust and rarely sets flower buds. Partly frosted growth sometimes looks diseased with distorted, puckered, one-sided or even chlorotic leaves.

Chlorosis

This can develop for various reasons, such as inadequate drainage or exceptionally wet or dry seasons or from an imbalance of plant nutrients. It is very hard to recognise the various deficiencies or toxicities from the type of chlorosis present. If too much lime is not suspected, it is advisable to have the soil analysed and to get other professional advice.

Snow damage

Really heavy snowfalls, or late wet snow, can break branches of rhododendrons. Well grown, sturdy bushes with compact growth can usually withstand the weight, but open or leggy specimens may not be able to tolerate being bent right over. It is hard to know whether the snow should be shaken off or not. However, low growing and young plants are well protected from frost by heavy snowfalls and therefore all snow should definitely be left on these.

Climate problems

HARDINESS

This is a subject that we are always learning more about. No two seasons are really alike and, as a result, all plants including rhododendrons respond differently.

Damage from frost can be divided into two types: seasonable mid-winter frosts and unseasonable early autumn and late spring ones. The amount of damage caused by early and late spring frosts depends on the condition of the plants. In this country, there are very many rhododendron species and hybrids which can withstand almost any winter low temperature that we can

The blood-red forms of the magnificent *Rhododendron arboreum* (p.47) are not reliably hardy outside the mildest districts

experience, *provided* that they are dormant. It is the unseasonable frosts which cause so many failures (see bark split and frosted young growth, p.42). Alternating warm and cold spells in winter result in the trusses of many rhododendrons opening with a few buds per truss destroyed.

A few people take no chances and grow only the toughest possible varieties, but many of these lack the interest and charm of the more tender ones. Surely it is worth taking a gamble! Given good growing conditions, many slightly vulnerable varieties will recover from any minor set-backs.

What can be done to alleviate frost damage? Shade and shelter are mentioned on p.14. The use of fertilizers for hardening off is dealt with on p.26. Well-grown bushes which have not been over-fed with fertilizers are those most likely to withstand severe weather conditions. There is no doubt that overhead tree cover does give considerable protection in late spring and early autumn especially. Glass or plastic cloches (not polythene) are certainly beneficial to young or dwarf varieties and those of suspect hardiness should always be given some protection for the first years of their lives. Many species are very much more tender in their immature state than after they reach 2 to 3 feet (60 to 90 cm) and have developed their full-sized, mature leaves. Other means of protection are cold frames, rings of wire netting filled with bracken fronds, dry straw or leaves, or a hat of evergreen foliage. But beware of rotting the plants underneath!

WHAT WILL GROW WHERE

From the point of view of rhododendron hardiness, this country can be divided roughly into three zones of hardiness, as follows:

1. The west and south coastal districts, especially islands and peninsulas. These are the most favoured areas for growing tender varieties, such as the big-leaved species and the scented varieties. Much shelter is generally needed.

2. East and south-east coastal areas and low lying areas inland. Here much depends on the local situation. Bad frost pockets are only suitable for cast-iron or late flowering varieties, but other more desirable sites will satisfy all but the most tender. Most of the Kurume azaleas are only good in southern districts.

3. All high ground above approximately 500 feet (150 m). Here the growing season is shorter with more early and late frosts. Select hardy varieties. With good shelter and air drainage (from frost i.e. avoiding frost pockets), conditions can be surprisingly good. Evergreen azaleas are seldom satisfactory.

Species and hybrid descriptions

There is now a vast array of both species and hybrids to choose from. In this book, a selection of the best is given. These include many of the old favourites and the best known modern varieties, plus a few which are still rare and only occasionally obtainable from nurseries, but which are of special merit. However, the selection which follows is, to some extent, a personal one.

Nearly all species and many hybrid groups show great variability in growth and flower. In certain cases this amounts to excellent, good, bad and indifferent forms. In varieties that are easy to propagate regularly there is no excuse for the distribution of poor forms but occasionally this does still happen. Only the better forms (clones) should be bought and, with those species hard to propagate, hand pollinated seedlings from good stock are often the best that can be obtained. Do not be tempted into buying bargain lots and if possible see the plants in flower at the nursery.

For simplification of choice, species and hybrids are grouped into four heights plus the tender varieties.

To express the varying merits of the plants the following symbols are used for their characters, with further subdivisions by number:

H = Hardiness: five hardiness groups are designated from 1 to 5; the higher the number the hardier the plant.

H5 hardy in inland glens and all other coldest areas.
H4 hardy in other inland areas.
H3 suitable for the west, and for sheltered areas near the south and east coast.
H2 for very sheltered gardens on the west coast.
H1 for greenhouse or sheltered walls.

F = Flower
L = Leaf

Qualifications given to plants for flower and leaf value are also numbered 1 to 5. The higher the number the better and 5 is excellent. In the lists below the months given are those of flowering.

The Royal Horticultural Society gives awards to plants which are considered to be especially noteworthy. These are given below (with date of award and flower colour) to help in selecting the better forms of the species. The following awards are given to individual clones only and do not apply to every plant of a species or hybrid grex group:

F.C.C   First Class Certificate, the highest award.
A.M.   Award of Merit.

RHODODENDRON SPECIES FOR OUTDOORS

Tall

15 ft (4.6 m) or more. To grow well, these require shelter and some shade.

R. arboreum H2–4 F2–4 (Jan. Apr.) L3–4
One of the few rhododendrons that often develops a single trunk and can reach 40 ft (12 m) or more in favoured localities. A very variable species. Rigid leaves up to 8 in. (20 cm) long, white, fawn, cinnamon to rusty brown below. Flowers in dense rounded trusses, blood-red, pink to white, sometimes spotted. The blood-red forms are the most tender, and can only be grown in really mild areas. Very showy in full flower, and variable in hardiness.

R.barbatum H3–4 F2–4 (Mar.) L2–3
Develops into a nicely shaped large bush if given space. Leaves up to 8 in. (20 cm) long; leaf stalks and branchlets usually clad with long bristles. Flowers in round compact trusses, of a fine scarlet. Rather early flowering. Very decorative bark. Hardy in most areas of Britain.

R. decorum H3–4 F2–3 (May June) L2–3
In the hardier forms, this is the most generally suitable of the larger species for growing all over the country. Leaves up to 6 in. (15 cm) long. Flowers in a flat-topped truss, white to shell pink with or without spots, scented. Very easily grown and is one of the most lime tolerant species.

R.oreodoxa and var. *fargesii* H4 F2–4 (Mar.Apr.) L2–3
One of the most free flowering of the larger species. Neat leaves up to 3½ in. (9 cm) long. Flowers in loose trusses, bell-shaped, rose to white, with or without spots. Very hardy and easily grown. Quite tolerant of lime.

R. rex ssp. *fictolacteum* H4 F2–4 (Apr. May) L2–3
The best of this type for colder gardens. Excellent dark green foliage with buff to rusty indumentum below, most attractive with the sun on it. Compact trusses of white to rose tinted flowers with a dark crimson blotch, 2 in. (5 cm) long.

R. rubiginosum H4 F2–3 (Mar. May) L1–2
This attractive, free flowering, comparatively small-leaved species stands up well to wind and is good for interior windbreaks. Dark green leaves up to 2½ in. (6 cm) long, rust coloured below. Flowers funnel-shaped, rosy lilac, pink to almost white, spotted brown. Grows quite well on lime.

R. thomsonii H4 F3–4 (Mar. May) L2–3
Magnificent when covered with deep blood-red waxy flowers. The leaves in many forms have a glaucous bloom above and the bark is smooth and peeling. Leaves up to 3½ in. (9 cm) long. Flowers in loose trusses. Susceptible to powdery mildew.

Medium

8–15 ft (2.4–4.6 m). Best grown under woodland conditions or where there is some shade and shelter. This group includes nearly all the Triflora subsection which have rather thin branches, small scaly leaves, and plentifully produced butterfly-like flowers in small trusses.

R. augustinii H3–4 F2–4 (Apr. May) L1–2
The nearest to blue of the larger species. A Triflorum. Very effective in masses. Leaves up to 5 in. (13 cm) long. Flowers usually pale lavender-blue to intense violet. The deepest blue forms are the most tender. The others will grow in most parts of Britain, but all are liable to bark split after unseasonable late frosts. They are quite lime tolerant.

R. campanulatum H3–4 F1–4 (Apr. May) L2–4
A very variable species with many different forms in cultivation. Leaves up to 6 in. (15 cm) long, dark glossy green above, and clad underneath with thick to thin fawn to rusty brown indumentum. The flowers are in compact or loose trusses in many shades of purple, mauve, rosy white or white, usually well spotted. Often a fine foliage plant as well. Most introductions are hardy but some suffer from bark split after late frosts.

R. campylocarpum H3–4 F3–4 (Apr.) L2
One of the finest yellow flowered species. Leaves up to 4 in. (10 cm) long, dark glossy green above. Flowers in loose trusses, bell-shaped, canary-yellow to pale yellow. Suitable for all but the very coldest gardens in Britain.

R.cinnabarinum H3–4 F3–4 (Apr. July) L2–3
A most unusual and beautiful species with waxy, tubular, mostly pendant flowers. Many forms occur with different leaves, flowers and times of flowering. Leaves up to 3 in. (8 cm) long, glaucous to dark green above. Flowers in small loose trusses, cinnabar, red, crimson, pale pinkish purple, plum purple, yellow or orange or with a combination of red, yellow and apricot. Most forms are fairly hardy but some are subject to bark split and subsequent die-back. Susceptible to powdery mildew.

R. oreotrephes H4 F2–3 (Apr. May) L1–3
A beautiful plant (Triflora subsection), in the best forms with fine glaucous young foliage and lovely rose pink flowers. Leaves up to 4½ in. (11 cm) long, usually much less, sometimes semi-deciduous. Flowers mauve-pink, purple or rose, rarely white. Best grown in an open, fairly sunny position to keep it compact.

R. souliei H4–5 F2–4 (May) L2–3
One of the most beautiful of all species. Almost round leaves up to 3 in. (8 cm) long. Lovely, saucer-shaped flowers, soft or deeper rose or white, 2 in. (5 cm) or more across. Does best in dry cold areas.

R. wardii H4 F2–4 (May June) L2–3
A first class yellow-flowered species, very variable. Leaves up to 4 in. (10 cm) long. Flowers in loose trusses, saucer-shaped, bright or clear lemon-yellow, sometimes with a crimson blotch. Some of the Ludlow and Sherriff introductions are especially good.

R. yunnanense H3–4 F2–4 (May) L1–2
An exceedingly valuable species of the Triflora subsection, which should be in every garden. Leaves up to 4 in. (10 cm) long. Flowers funnel-shaped in pink, white, pale rose-lavender or lavender. Always smothers itself in flower from an early age and is easily grown. Quite hardy but is occasionally liable to bark split from a late frost.

Low

4–8 ft (1.22–2.44 m). For near the front of borders or light woodland.

R. *aberconwayi* H4 F2–4 (May June) L1–2
In the best forms, this is a beautiful species. Leaves up to 4 in. (10 cm) long, with a hard and thick texture. Flowers white or white tinged pink, more or less spotted with crimson, flat in upstanding trusses.

R.*bureavii* H4–5 F2–3 (Apr. May) L3–4
One of the finest foliage plants in the genus. Leaves up to 5 in. (13 cm) long, thick and leathery; the underside and branchlets are covered with thick rusty red woolly indumentum. Flowers in compact trusses, white or rose with crimson markings, up to 2 in. (5 cm) long. Slow to flower.

R. *callimorphum* H3–4 F3–4 (May June) L2–3
A first-rate species for the small garden. Leaves up to 3 in. (8 cm) long, almost round. Flowers soft to deep rose in a loose truss. The lovely flowers, freely produced, are set off well by the attractive foliage. Worth trying in any sheltered position but liable to bark split.

R. *ciliatum* H3–4 F2–3 (Mar. Apr.) L1–2
An attractive early, free-flowering species, unfortunately very easily frosted. Leaves up to 3½ in. (9 cm) long, hairy. Flowers white or pink tinged, narrowly bell-shaped, up to 2 in. (5 cm) across. Good for edging a border. Not suitable for the coldest gardens. Moderately lime tolerant.

R. *dauricum* H4–5 F2–3 (Jan. Mar.) L1–2
The earliest species to flower. Leaves up to 1½ in. (4 cm) long, semi-evergreen or deciduous. Flowers bright rose-purple to bright purple or rarely pink or white, surprisingly frost hardy. They are very freely produced and it is a real harbinger of spring. The closley related R. *mucronulatum* has longer leaves.

R. *degronianum* H4–5 F1–3 (Apr. May) L2–3
A neat plant, often compact. Leaves up to 6 in. (15 cm) long, with fawn to rufous indumentum below. Flowers in loose trusses, clear soft pink with deeper lines, up to 2½ in. (6 cm) across. Desirable in the better forms. Now includes R. *metternichii*.

R. *dichroanthum* H3–4 F1–3 (May June) L1–2
A very variable species, well worth growing the best orange-flowered introductions. Leaves up to 4 in. (10 cm) long, with white, grey or fawn indumentum below. Flowers deep or dull orange to salmon-pink or yellowish copper.

R. *glaucophyllum* H4 F2–3 (Apr. May) L1–2
A very free flowering species with aromatic foliage. Leaves up to 3½ in. (9 cm) long, glaucous white underneath. Flowers bell-shaped in a loose truss, pink, rose or pinkish purple, rarely white. Excellent for the edge of woodland. Var. *tubiforme* flowers more tubular.

R. *haematodes* H4–5 F3–4 (May June) L2–3
A first-class species with neat attractive foliage. Leaves up to 3 in. (7.5 cm) long, dark green above. Both young shoots and leaf undersides are covered with dense woolly indumentum. Flowers fleshy, brilliant scarlet-crimson to scarlet, in loose trusses, up to 2 in. (5 cm) long. A little slow to flower but well worth waiting for. Quite hardy.

R. *neriiflorum* H3–4 F3–4 (Apr. May) L1–2
One of the best red, scarlet or crimson species. Leaves up to 4 in. (10 cm) long.

49

Flowers waxy, in loose trusses, up to 2 in. (5 cm) long. Many forms are unfortunately only suited to mild areas but selected introductions are reasonably hardy. Very variable.

R.orbiculare H4 F2–3 (Mar. Apr.) L2–3
A lovely foliage plant when well grown. Leaves up to 4 in. (10 cm) long, almost round, bright green. Flowers rose-pink to rose in loose trusses. To develop a perfect dome-shaped specimen, do not plant in too much shade and allow plenty of room.

R.pseudochrysanthum H4–5 F3–4 (Apr.) L2–3
A fine species now becoming better known. Leaves densely crowded, up to 3 in. (7.5 cm) long, thick and leathery with indumentum on the midrib below. Flowers pale pink to white with rose lines and crimson spots, up to 2 in. (5 cm) long. Usually compact, with nice, unusual foliage and most attractive flowers.

R. racemosum H4 F1–3 (Mar. Apr.) L1–2
A most adaptable species, occuring in many forms from dwarf up to 10 ft (3 m). Leaves up to 2 in. (5 cm) long, very glaucous below. Flowers axillary, often all up at the top 3–4 in. (7.5–10 cm) of the shoots; pink, pale to deep rose or white, up to nearly 1 inch (2.5 cm) long. The best dwarf forms grow under the collector's number Forrest 19404. A.M 1970 'Rock Rose'; F.C.C. 1892.

R. roxieanum H5 F2–3 (Apr. May) L2–3
Most unusual narrow leaves and pretty little compact trusses of white flushed pink flowers. Leaves up to $4\frac{3}{4}$ inch (12 cm) long, flowers about $1\frac{1}{4}$ in. (3 cm) long, can be slow to bloom. Very variable.

Rhododendron augustinii (p.48), a variable Chinese species which can have almost blue flowers

Above: *Rhododendron aberconwayi* (p.49) likes a fairly sunny position
Below: the distinctive leaves of *Rhododendron orbiculare* set off the
bell-shaped flowers

R. *tsariense* H4 F2–3 (Mar. May) L2–3
Lovely foliage with rusty indumentum on lower and upper sides and fairylike flowers. Leaves up to 2½ in. (6 cm) long, Flowers white flushed pink, spotted, about 1½ in. (3 cm) long. 'Yum-Yum' A.M. 1964.

Dwarfs

4 ft (1.2 m) and under. For rock gardens and peat borders in at least half sunshine, especially in the north.

R. *calostrotum* H4–5 F2–4 (May) L1–3
One of the most beautiful of all the dwarfs. Leaves usually glaucous green above, up to 1⅓ in. (3.5 cm) long. Flowers bright rose-crimson to rich purple. Almost flat, and large for the size of the plant; very freely produced. F.C.C. 1971 'Gigha', bright rose-crimson; A.M. 1935 deep rosy mauve to magenta form. Ssp. *riparioides* taller with larger blue-purple flowers. Calciphilum Group smaller leaves and pink flowers.

R. *calostrotum* ssp. *keleticum* Radicans Group H4 F2–3 (May June) L1–2
A creeping mat-like shrub with the flowers held well above the foliage. Leaves up to ¾ inch (2 cm) long, shiny above. Flowers almost flat, pale to dark purple, ¾ inch (2 cm) long. An excellent ground cover for peat walls and useful for the lateness of the flowers. A.M. 1926, rosy purple flowers, 1 inch (2.5 cm) across.

R. *campylogynum* H3–4 F2–3 (May June) L2–3
A very variable species with the neatest little thimble-like flowers on long flower stalks. Leaves up to 1 in. (2.5 cm) long, usually glaucous below. Flowers claret, salmon-pink to pale rose-purple or black-purple, or cream coloured. Gems for the rock garden. Nearly all are hardy. A.M. 1973 white form. Myrtilloides Group very dwarf with small flowers; Charopoeum Group the largest flowered variety; Celsum Group the tallest, with erect habit; Cremastum Group leaves green underneath, of which 'Bodnant Red' A.M. 1971 is a good clone.

R. *camtschaticum* H4–5 F2–3 (May) L1–2
A most unusual deciduous species. Leaves up to 2 in. (5 cm) long, hairy. Flowers reddish purple, red, pink or rarely white spotted, nearly flat, about 1½ in. (4 cm) across. Easily grown in Scotland but more difficult in the south of England. Grow in full sun in the north.

R. *cephalanthum* H4 F2–3 (Apr. May) L1–2
Delightful small trusses of daphne-like tubular flowers. Leaves up to 1½ in. (14 cm) long, aromatic. Flowers white or pink, up to ¾ in. (2 cm) long. Excellent for rock-gardens or peat walls. Crebreflorum Group is one of the loveliest of all dwarfs. Very low, with pink flowers.

R. *rupicola* var. *chryseum* H4 F2–3 (Apr. May) L1–2
One of the few yellow Lapponicums, which looks excellent grown alongside the other predominantly mauve to blue species. Leaves up to ½ in. (1.5 cm) long. Flowers pale to bright yellow. Hardy in most forms.

R. *ferrugineum* H4–5 F1–2 (June) L1–2
The well known dwarf from the Alps of Europe. Leaves up to 1½ in. (4 cm) long. Flowers tubular, rosy crimson or white. Very hardy. A.M. 1969 *ferrugineum album* white flowers. The similar R.*hirsutum* will grow on moderately alkaline soils.

R. *forrestii* H4 F1–4 (Mar.May) L1–2
When well flowered, this is quite one of the finest dwarfs, but many forms rarely flower. Leaves up to 1½ in. (4 cm) long, purple underneath. Flowers bright scarlet,

tubular, waxy. Repens Group is the more usual variety, of which the best form is Rock 59174. Leaves green underneath, prostrate habit. F.C.C. 1935. Tumescens Group dome shaped habit. All are hardy except for the young growth; some shade is needed.

R. hippophaeoides H4–5 F2–3 (Mar. May) L2–3
A handsome easily grown rather upright semi-dwarf, growing up to 5 ft (1.5 m). Leaves up to 1¼ in. (3 cm) long, slightly glaucous green. Flowers usually lavender-blue. A.M. 1927 lavender-blue. Fairly lime tolerant.

R. impeditum H4–5 F3–4 (Apr. May) L2–3
One of the best dwarfs for general garden use. Leaves about ½ in. (1.3 cm) long. Flowers mauve or light purplish blue, about ⅔ in. (1.6 cm) long. Similar to R. fastigiatum but even more compact with less glaucous leaves. Very hardy and free flowering. A.M. 1944.

R. keiskei H4–5 F2–3 (Mar. May) L1–2
One of the hardiest cream to yellow dwarfs, often with attractive bronzy young growth. Variable. Leaves up to 2½ in. (6 cm) long, flowers about 1 in. (2.5 cm) long. 'Yaku Fairy' A.M. 1970 is a splendid prostrate form, May flowering. A.M. 1929 to a pale yellow form.

R. lepidostylum H4–5 F1 (May June) L3–4
The finest glaucous foliage plant among the dwarfs. Leaves especially blue when young, about 1½ in. (4 cm) long. Flowers yellow, often hidden in the foliage. Should be in every garden. A.M. 1969 for foliage.

R. orthocladum var. microleucum H4–5 F3 (Apr.) L2
Pretty little pure white flowers which contrast well with the earlier mauve and blue varieties. Leaves up to ⅔ in. (1.6 cm) long. Surprisingly frost resistant flowers. F.C.C. 1939.

R. moupinense H4 F3–4 (Feb. Mar.) L1–2
A lovely harbinger of spring, well worth the risk of frost. Leaves up to 1½ in. (4 cm) long, shiny above, thick and leathery. Flowers white, pink or deep rose. Best planted under trees away form the early morning sun. Hardy when mature but likes perfect drainage. A.M. 1914 white flowers 2 in. (5 cm) across; A.M 1937 flowers heavily suffused with rose-pink. Drought resistant.

R. pemakoense H4 F2–3 (Mar. Apr.) L1–2
Mases of comparatively large flowers can completely hide the foliage in favourable seasons. Leaves up to 1¼ in. (3 cm) long. Flowers pale pinkish purple to pale purple, up to 1½ in. (4 cm) long. Easily grown, but the flower buds are often frosted. Sometimes stoloniferous. Hardy as a plant. A.M. 1933, white flowers suffused with mauve.

R. polycladum H4 F2–4 (Apr. May) L1–2
In the best forms, this is the nearest to a true blue of all rhododendrons. Leaves up to ½ in. (1.3 cm) long. Flowers very freely produced, lavender to almost a royal blue, about ½ in. (1.3 cm) long. F.C.C. 1934, lavender-blue; A.M. 1924, purplish rose.

R. russatum H4 F3–4 (Apr. May) L1–2
The finest species of this colour in the genus with bright deep reddish to blue-purple flowers. Leaves about 1 in. (2.5 cm) long. F.C.C. 1933, intense purple; A.M. 1927, violet-blue.

R. sargentianum H4 F2–3 (Apr. May) L1-2
One of the neatest dwarfs with charming little cream to yellow flowers. Leaves up

The flowers of *Rhododendron yakushimanum* become pure white when fully expanded

to $\frac{3}{4}$ in. (2 cm) long. Flowers about $\frac{1}{4}$ (1.3 cm) across. Very compact habit. Hardy, and slow growing. Appreciates a little shade. A.M. 1923, pale yellow; A.M. 1966, 'Whitebait', cream.

R. trichostomum H3–4 F2–3 (May June) L1–2
Round trusses of pink, rose or white flowers, most showy, long lasting and attractive in the best selections. Leaves up to $1\frac{1}{3}$ in. (2 cm) long. A few forms are rather tender. F.C.C. 1976. 'Collingwood Ingram', rose suffused white, A.M. 1960.

R. williamsianum H4 F2–3 (Apr.) L2–3
A beautiful dome-shaped shrub with lovely bell-shaped flowers, showing up well against the nearly round leaves. Leaves up to $1\frac{3}{4}$ in. (4.5 cm) long. Hardy as a plant but the pretty young growth gets frosted in some areas. A.M. 1938.

R. yakushimanum H4–5 F3–4 (May) L2–3
Perhaps the most sought-after of all rhododendron species. Pale pink flowers, fading to white, in compact trusses over fine dark foliage on a perfect dome-shaped bush. Leaves about $3\frac{1}{2}$ in. (9 cm) long, recurved, with thick, light buff indumentum below. F.C.C. 1947.

TENDER RHODODENDRON SPECIES

For indoors or very mild sheltered gardens.

R. edgeworthii H2–3 F2–4 (Apr. May) L3–4
One of the best scented species. Lovely flowers and fine foliage. Height occasionally to 10 ft (3 m), often straggly. Leaves about 4 in. (10 cm) long, dark green and rough above; cobwebby indumentum below. Flowers 4 in. (10 cm) across, white or tinged pink, deliciously fragrant. Some forms are hardy in a well sheltered garden if given perfect drainage. F.C.C. 1933.

R. formosum H2–3 F2–3 (May June)
Height to 6 ft (2 m), often straggly. Leaves about 2 in. (5 cm) long, hairy. Flowers white or white tinged pink, slightly scented. A.M. 1960. Var. *inaequale* has larger leaves and larger, deliciously scented flowers, but is more tender. F.C.C. 'Elizabeth Bennet' 1981.

R. lindleyi H1–3 F4 (Apr. May) L2–3
Beautiful large scented flowers; a wonderful plant. Height to 15 ft (4.5 m), unfortunately of rather a leggy habit. Leaves up to 6 in. (15 cm) long. Flowers white or cream with a yellow blotch, sometimes flushed with rose, almost lily-shaped, about 5 in. (12 cm) across. The Ludlow and Sherriff introduction is the hardiest, but most will survive in warm, west-coast gardens.

R. maddenii ssp. *crassum* H2–3 F2–3 (June July) L2–3
One of the hardiest of the strongly scented species. Height to 15 ft (4.5 m) often less. Leaves up to 5 in. (12 cm) long, dark green, glossy and thick. Flowers white, or white tinged pink. Reasonably hardy in very sheltered gardens. A.M. 1924, white flowers.

Vireya (Malesian) rhododendrons

This group comes from the tropical regions between Malaya and North Queensland, Australia. They are not used to winter and summer seasons and therefore cannot tolerate our cold winters. Many species occur and most of these can be grown successfully in pots or very carefully drained beds in a frost-free greenhouse. Flower size varies from small narrow tubes to large and showy. Nearly all tend to be rather straggly in habit and vary in height from a few inches to many feet. Several are scented.

Over half a century ago these were popular indoor plants and many hybrids were raised, known as Javanese hybrids. Their popularity died out and so did many of the cultivars grown. Many hitherto unknown species are being introduced from Borneo and New Guinea. Very few are at present available from nurseries, but if interest in these plants increases, the finest species and hybrids may become obtainable. Many are very beautiful and are well worth a place in a cool house.

Amongst the best species are *R. christianae*, deep yellow, shaded orange; *R. gracilentum*, pink or red, dwarf; *R. javanicum*, yellow to scarlet; *R. konori*, white; *R. laetum*, deep yellow; and *R. lochae*, scarlet.

RHODODENDRON HYBRIDS

In the table which follows the names indented are those of clones that belong to the grex, and the figures for hardiness and flower value and the months of flowering are the same as for the grex: the clones may differ in merit and flower colour.

Name	H	F	Flower colour	Time
Tall: 12 feet (3.6 m) or more				
A. Bedford	4	3	lavender, deep blotch	June
Betty Wormald	4	4	pink	May–June
Crest	4	5	yellow	May
Cynthia	5	4	rose-crimson	May–June
Fastuosum Flore Pleno	5	4	mauve, double	June
Lem's Monarch	4	5	pink, light centre	May
Loderi				
King George	3–4	5	pink, fading to white	May–June
Pink Diamond	3–4	5	pink	May–June
Venus	3–4	5	pale pink	May–June
Mother of Pearl	4	4	pink to white	May–June
Pink Pearl	4	4	rose-pink	May–June
Polar Bear	4	4	white, scented	July–August
Sappho	5	3	white, dark blotch	May–June
Medium: 6–12 ft (1.8–3.6 m)				
David	4	4	blood red	May
Furnivall's Daughter	4	5	pink, large blotch	May–June
Goldsworth Orange	4	3	orange	June–July
Gomer Waterer	5	3	blush white	July
Hotei	3–4	5	deep yellow	May
Jean Marie de				
Montague	4	4	scarlet	late May
Lady Chamberlain	3–4	4	orange salmon	May
Lady Rosebery	3–4	4	pink	May
Lavender Girl	4	3	lavender	May–June
Loders White	3–4	5	pale pink to white	May
Mrs A.T. de la Mare	5	3	white	May–June
Naomi				
Exbury Naomi	4	4	lilac/yellow	May
Nautilus	4	4	rose flushed orange	May
Nobleanum	4	3	crimson scarlet	Dec–April
Nova Zembla	5	3	red	May–June
Purple Splendour	4	4	deep purple	June
Scintillation	5	4	pastel pink, brown marks	May–June
Susan	4	4	lavender	May
Tortoiseshell (several)	3–4	2–4	yellow to scarlet	June
Trude Webster	5	5	pink	May–June
Virginia Richards	4	4	pink to yellowish	May–June
Low: 4–6 ft (1.2–1.8 m)				
Anna Baldsiefen	4	4	bright pink	April
Blue Diamond	4	4	blue	April–May
Bow Bells	4	3	pink	May
Britannia	4	4	crimson-red	May
Christmas Cheer	5	3	blush pink	Feb–April
Doncaster	4	3	scarlet-crimson	May–June
Dopey	4	4	deep red	May–June
Elizabeth	4	5	blood-red	April–May
Fabia	3–4	3	orange-salmon	May–June
Fabia Tangerine	3–4	3	orange-red	May–June
Helen Schiffner	4	4	pure white	May–June
Hydon Dawn	4	4	pink fading	May–June
May Day	3–4	3	scarlet	May–June
Percy Wiseman	5	4	peach-pink and cream	May–June

Name	H	F	Flower colour	Time
P.J. Mezitt	5	4	deep lavender-pink	April–May
Praecox	4	3	rosy-purple	March-April
Seta	3–4	4	white flushed pink	March–April
Snow Lady	3–4	4	white	March–April
Surrey Heath	4	4	salmon-rose, cream centre	May–June
Unique	4	4	pale ochre or yellow	April–May
Vanessa F.C.C.	3–4	4	pink	June
Vanessa Pastel	3–4	4	creamy-peach	June
Vintage Rose	4	5	clear pink fading	May–June
Winsome	3–4	3	rosy-cerise	May
Yellow Hammer	3–4	3	yellow	March-April

Dwarfs: up to 4 ft (1.2 m)

Name	H	F	Flower colour	Time
Arctic Tern	5	4	pure white	May
Carmen	4	3	dark red	April–May
Chikor	4	4	yellow	April–May
Cilpinense	3–4	4	pink	March-April
Curlew	4	5	yellow	May
Creeping Jenny	3–4	3	blood-red	April–May
Dora Amateis	5	4	opening white	April–May
Ginny Gee	4	4	pink and white	April–May
Linda	5	3	rose-red	May
Pink Drift	5	3	pinkish-mauve	May
Princess Anne	4	4	yellow	May
Ptarmigan	4	4	white	April-May
Ramapo	5	3	pale violet	April–May
Razorbill	4	5	brightest pink	April–May
Riplet	4	4	deep rose fading to cream	April
Sarled	4	3	pale pink to white	May–June
Scarlet Wonder	5	4	bright red	May
Snipe	4	3	pink	April–May
Songbird	4	4	blue-violet	April–May

Tender hybrids

Only suitable for indoors in all but the mildest sheltered western seaboard gardens or on a very protected partially shaded wall.

'Fragrantissimum' (H1–2: F4) is the best known scented hybrid. White flowers tinged pink. Still well worth growing. F.C.C. 1868. Rather similar are 'Lady Alice Fitzwilliam' and 'Princess Alice'.

Azaleodendrons

These are crosses between evergreen rhododendrons and deciduous azaleas. The foliage tends to be sparse and semi-evergreen. While interesting, their merit does not equal the best typical rhododendrons or azaleas. Two examples are Broughtonii Aureum (H4:F3) semi-deciduous with yellow flowers, F.C.C. 1935; and Martha Isaacson (H4:F4) beautiful white with crimson stripes.

There is also a group of hybrids, recently raised, between R. racemosum and Obtsusum azaleas. These are very free flowering and quite showy. An example is Martine (H4:F4) masses of shell pink flowers in May; rather pale leaves.

57

Above: Loderi (p.56), a famous hybrid with many forms, raised at
Leonardslee in Sussex
Below: the eye-catching yellow flowers of 'Hotei' (p.56)

Above: 'Percy Wiseman' (p.57) received a First Class Certificate in 1986 after trial at Wisley
Below: the glistening flowers of 'Riplet' (p.57) are freely produced early in the season

AZALEA SPECIES

Deciduous

R. *albrechtii* H4 F3–4 (Apr. May) L1–2
In the best deep coloured forms, this is one of the loveliest of all the azaleas. Height to 10 ft (3 m). Flowers nearly flat, deep rose pink, or light purplish rose, with olive-green spots. Winter hardy but young growth is liable to be frosted. F.C.C. 1962, 'Michael McLaren'.

R. *atlanticum* H5 F2–3 (May) L1–3
A low-growing, sometimes stoloniferous azalea with pretty tubular flowers. Height to 3 ft (90 cm). Leaves up to 2½ in. (6 cm) long, often glaucous above. Flowers white or white flushed pink or purple, fragrant. A.M. 1965, 'Seaboard' white flushed pale pink.

R. *calendulaceum* H5 F2–4 (May June) L1–2
A wonderful azalea in the best orange or scarlet forms. Height to 15 ft (4.57 m). Leaves up to 3½ in. (9 cm) long. Flowers variable, yellow to orange or scarlet or salmon-pink, about 2 in. (5 cm) across. Hardy and reliable. A.M. 1965 'Burning Light' coral-red.

R. *luteum* (*flavum* or *Azalea pontica*) H5 F3–4 (May) L2–3
The common yellow azalea. Leaves up to 4 in. (10 cm) long. Height to 12 ft (3.6 m), usually less. The flowers are very fragrant, about 2 in. (5 cm) across. Valuable for its autumn colour. Still regarded as a garden plant of great merit.

R. *occidentale* H4 F2–4 (June Aug.) L1–3
One of the finest azaleas, especially in the carefully selected forms and strains now being introduced from western U.S.A. Height to 10 ft (3 m). Flowers up to 5 in. (12.5 cm) across, in various shades of cream to pink, often flushed or blotched; sweetly scented. The foliage sometimes colours well. A.M. 1944, white with yellow blotch, flushed rose-pink.

R. *prinophyllum* H5 F2–3 (May) L1–2
A dainty species, with tubular flowers of clear pink in the best forms. Height occasionally to 12 ft (3.6 m), usually much less. Very hardy. A.M. 1955, phlox pink.

R. *schlippenbachii* H4–5 F3–4 (Apr. May) L2–3
A charming azalea with large flat-shaped flowers and nice foliage. Flowers very pale pink to rose pink with reddish spots, up to 3½ in. (9 cm) across. Hardy but the young growth can be frosted. Height to about 6 ft (2 m). F.C.C. 1944 rose-pink; F.C.C. 1965, 'Prince Charming', bright rose-pink.

R. *vaseyi* H4 F2–4 (Apr. May) L2–3
Another first class azalea. Height to about 8 ft (2.4 m) but occasionally more. Flowers rose pink to white. Hardy and reliable. A.M. 1969 'Suva'.

R. *viscosum* H5 F2–3 (June–July) L1–2
Useful for its lateness and hardiness. White or white suffused pink flowers, narrowly tubular, with a strong spicy scent. A.M. 1921. There are several good new hybrids of this.

Evergreen

R. *indicum* H2–3 F2–3 (June) L1–2
A rather tender species, only suited to the hottest and mildest parts of the country. Often low growing or prostrate. Leaves evergreen. Flowers red to scarlet or rose

red, about 2½ in. (6 cm) across. Useful for its late flowering. Is the parent of many hybrids including the Satsuki group. 'Balsaminaeflorum' (roseflora) a reasonably hardy low growing clone of the above with double salmon-red flowers (F3). The 'Azalea indica' of florists is not this species, but belongs to R. simsii and its hybrids.

R. *kaempferi* H4 F3–4 (May June) L1–2
Erect growing, often reaching over 5 ft (1.5 m). Leaves semi-evergreen. Flowers salmon-red, orange-red, pink to rosy scarlet. This very hardy attractive and reliable plant is the parent of many of our best hybrids, suited to cold districts (see p.63). F.C.C. 1955 'Eastern Fire' with camellia-rose coloured flowers.

R. *kiusianum* H4 F1–3 (May) L1–2
An excellent hardy, low growing species, useful as a ground cover. Leaves semi-deciduous. Flowers purple, mauve, also rose-red and pink or rarely white. May be a parent of some of the Kurume azaleas (see p. 63).

R. *nakaharae* H4 F2–3 (June Aug.) L1–2
A first-class creeping, mat-forming dwarf. Leaves evergreen. Flowers brick-red to rose-red. A new introduction from Taiwan, with flowers produced late in the season. Seems to be quite hardy. A.M. 'Mariko' 1970.

R. *poukhanense* H4 F2–3 (Apr. May) L1–2
The hardiest of these azaleas. Leaves almost deciduous. Flowers rose to lilac-purple, quite large, fragrant, 2 in. (5 cm) across. Free flowering and showy.

AZALEA HYBRIDS

Ghent and Rustica azaleas

Small flowered singles or hose-in-hose, with attractive colours and a sweet scent. June. All are F4.

Coccinea Speciosa brilliant orange red.
Daviesii white flowers with a pale yellow eye.
Nancy Waterer golden yellow, deep eye.
Narcissiflora pale yellow double flowers. A.M. 1954, F.C.C. 1963.

Mollis azaleas

Large flowered with self colours. Usually sold as seedlings in mixed colours. Chiefly salmon, flame, pink, yellow, and cream. All are F4.

Christopher Wren orange-yellow flowers.
Dr M Oosthoek deep orange-red flowers. A.M. 1920 and 1940.
Spek's Orange orange flowers. A.M. 1948 F.C.C. 1953.

Occidentale hybrids

Late flowering in pale colours.

Irene Koster (F3) rose-pink, late.

Exbury and Knaphill azaleas

Large flowered hybrids derived from the crossing of many species. They have a wide range of colours. Often sold as seedlings, either to colour or mixed. Nearly all are good and they are excellent value for massing. All are hardy and are best grown in very light woodland. May–June.

Berryrose (F3) pink, yellow blotch. A.M 1934.
Cecile (F3) salmon-pink, yellow blotch.
George Reynolds (F4) buttercup-yellow, deeper blotch A.M. 1934.
Gibraltar (F4) orange.
Glowing Embers (F3) red, orange blotch.
Golden Sunset (F3) light yellow, orange blotch.
Homebush (F4) semi-double rose-pink A.M 1950.
Hotspur Red (F4) reddish-orange.
Klondyke (F3) golden-yellow.
Persil (F3) white, yellow blotch.
Royal Command (F3) vermilion.
Satan (F4) scarlet
Silver Slipper (F4) white flushed pink. A.M. 1962, F.C.C. 1963.
Strawberry Ice (F3) pale pink.
Tunis (F2) orange-red.

The trumpet-shaped blooms of 'Cecile' (p.61) are typical of the Exbury azaleas

'Hatsugiri', a Kurume azalea with a profusion of small, but richly coloured flowers

Obtusum hybrids

Always sold as named clones.

Kurumes. Mostly fairly low growing, with a dense habit. Flowers single or hose-in-hose, $\frac{1}{2}$–$1\frac{1}{2}$ in. (1.3–3.8 cm) across. Early and mid May. Many are not suitable for northern Britain where the summers are too cool to ripen the wood. Grow in full sun or very light shade in the south and full sun in the north where a border against a south or west wall is excellent.

Hatsugiri (H4 F3) purplish crimson flowers, low and compact. Quite hardy. A.M. 1956.
Hino Crimson (H4 F3) deep rose.
Hinodegiri (H3 F4) bright crimson. A.M. 1965.
Hinomayo (H4 F4) soft pink. F.C.C. 1945.
Vida Brown (H4 F4) rose-pink flowers, large, small bush. A.M. 1960.

Kaempferi hybrids. Taller, and more upright. Flowers single, $1\frac{1}{2}$–$2\frac{1}{2}$ in. (3.8–6.3 cm) across. Mid to late May. These are generally better plants for northern districts than the Kurumes and flower well most seasons in a sunny position. Most have a good autumn colour.

Addy Wery (H4 F4) bright scarlet. A.M. 1950.
Blaauw's Pink (H4 F3) soft pink, hose-in-hose.
Fedora (H4 F4) dark pink. F.C.C. 1960.
John Cairns (H4 F4) Indian red; excellent in the north. A.M. 1940.
Naomi (H4 F4) salmon-pink, late. H.C. 1964.
Willy (H4 F3) clear pink flowers. Very hardy, excellent in the north.

Other azalea hybrids

Amoenum (H3–4) rich magenta or rosy purple flowers, usually hose-in-hose, small. A little tender in the north.

Amoenum Coccineum unstable sport of above, live carmine-red.

Blue Danube (H4 F3) rich blue purple, May, F.C.C. 1975.

Chippewa (H4 F3) rose-pink flowers, very late, hardy.

Diamant hybrids lilac-pink, salmon-pink, rosy red, dwarf, very hardy.

Favorite (H4 F3) deep rose-pink.

Gaiety (H4 F4) glowing rich pink, very hardy.

Johanna (H4 F3) carmine-red, dark shiny leaves.

Mother's Day (H4 F4) red, semi-double. A.M. 1945.

Mucronatum (Ledifolia Alba) (H4 F4) still one of the best white flowered varieties. There are several varieties of this.

Orange Beauty (H4 F4) orange-pink, A.M. 1945.

Palestrina (H3–4 F4) pure white, faint green eye. Rather tender in Scotland. A.M. 1944. F.C.C. 1967.

Panda (H4 F4) new, pure white, low.

Rosebud (H4 F3) double rose-pink. F.C.C. 1975.

Squirrel (H4 F4) bright scarlet, late, hardy.

Stewartstonian (H4 F3) clear red. A.M. 1975.

Vuyk's Rosy Red (H4 F4) rose-red. A.M. 1962.

Vuyk's Scarlet (H4 F4) deep flowers, an excellent variety. A.M. 1959. F.C.C.1966.

The Gumpo and Satsuki groups, derived from R. indicum and R. eriocarpum, need hot sun to ripen the wood for good flower production, so are only suited to the warmest districts.

The tender indoor large flowered varieties are usually bought in flower during the winter months. There are many excellent varieties, and it is best to choose the colour that is personally preferred.

THE R.H.S. RHODODENDRON AND CAMELLIA GROUP

This group is for members of the Royal Horticultural Society with a special interest in rhododendrons and camellias. There is small extra subscription, which includes receipt of the year book, Rhododendrons with Magnolias and Camellias, and bulletin, and excursions are arranged to gardens where rhododendrons are grown. The secretary of the group is Mrs Betty Jackson, 2 Essex Court, Temple, London EC47 9AP.

The year books, published since 1946 by the Royal Horticultural Society, contain a great deal of information on rhododendrons and their cultivation. For information write to the Secretary, The Royal Horticultural Society, Vincent Square, London SW1P 2PE.

Those living in Scotland may be interested in joining the Scottish Rhododendron Society. The Secretary is Mrs Rorie Hereson, Kinniard House, 3 Drymen Wynd, Bearsden, Glasgow G61 2UB.